T0145153

Recollections OF MY Life

DIMITRI GIDASPOW

AuthorHouse™
1663 Liberty Drive
Bloomington, IN 47403
www.authorhouse.com
Phone: 833-262-8899

Because of the dynamic nature of the Internet, any web addresses or links contained in this book may have changed
since publication and may no longer be valid. The views expressed in this work are solely those of the author and do
not necessarily reflect the views of the publisher, and the publisher hereby disclaims any responsibility for them.

Any people depicted in stock imagery provided by Getty Images are models,
and such images are being used for illustrative purposes only.
Certain stock imagery © Getty Images.

This book is printed on acid-free paper.

ISBN: 978-1-6655-2249-6 (sc)
ISBN: 978-1-6655-2248-9 (e)

Library of Congress Control Number: 2021907433

Print information available on the last page.

Published by AuthorHouse 04/09/2021

authorHOUSE®

1

My Parents

My father was born in 1898 In Russia on the Volga river. He told me that his grandparents name was Lebedev, Swan, in English. The Russian ruler said there were too many people with the same name. So they changed their name to Gidasp after a near-by river.

My grandfather was a priest and was in charge of their town. He was executed by the red Army during the revolution because he disobeyed their order not to have processions or meetings. In the Greek Orthodox church all the people march around the church on Easter, the biggest holiday. For this he was chosen to be a saint by the church.

My father was drafted into the Russian army in his first year in college. Since he knew geometry he was put into the artillery. They stopped the Red Army from crossing the Volga for a month and made their way all the way to the Pacific Ocean, where an American ship allowed whoever wanted to go to the USA. My father did not to go because too many men ran to the ship and there was no room for him.

When he came home he had to take care of his younger brothers and a sister because his mother had died of Cholera. He went back to school to obtain a degree in agriculture, the only one he was allowed to get because his father had been a priest. There was a high demand for agriculture engineers. After graduation he was sent to teach nomads near Iran how to be farmers. He left soon after arriving there since the nomads did not want to be farmers. Due to the need for such engineers my father came to Ukraine, a country that fed most of Europe for hundreds of years. Its rich soil is the reason Hitler went to war with the Soviet Union.

My mother Tatiana was born in 1902 in Kiev, Ukraine. Her father was a general in the Russian army fighting the Bolshewiks who won the war. He needed to change his identity because he had fought on the losing side and would have been executed. On the way home he found a dead soldier and changed his name to that of the soldier. Then he went to a small town in Ukraine, Kobeliaki. This is where I was born on June 4, 1934. It was one year after Stalin starved the Ukraine to force it to create collective farms.

I lived with my grandparents until I was almost 7 years old, since my parents were working elsewhere.

My mother's father, on the left holding his daughter, Nina who is ten years older than I am and lives in Switzerland and his daughter, Ala who is 5 years older than I am and lives in Paris. I am the small boy.

(From Left) Our Uncle Grisha, the priest, my aunt Olga and her husband, Vladimir.
They helped us come to the USA.

My mother with her cat, Foxy in Northbrook, July 1978

2

My Mother, Her Sisters, Daughters and Me

My mother's older sister Ira married a famous geological engineer Arthur Lewenhaupt. He led the 1939 geophysical expedition to Siberia where they found a mammoth which the dogs could still eat. For this accomplishment he got a medal from Stalin.

My father came to Ukraine where he met my mother who was an entomologist. The rich soil in Ukraine gave rise to beetles that ate the crops. They needed to be stopped. So my parents got a job at an agricultural experimental station, called Veseliy Podol, near farms in Ukraine. There my mother, working with a chemist, developed and tested the Russian version of DDT. It killed all the bugs and saved the crops but the smell was bad and it also killed the birds. My mother, the chemist and her boss got a medal from Krushchev, then the boss of Ukraine and later the leader of Soviet Union. He told my mother to go back to school to get an advanced degree. When she was gone my father took care of me. I fed our pigs and got an infection by stepping on a nail. I almost lost my leg.

My mother's older sister Ira and her two daughters Nina and Ala spent the summers with us. In winter we went to visit them in their house in Moscow. I remember their house, the zoo and great movies about the Russian authors.

Nina now lives in Switzerland. She is ten year older than I. Ala lives in Paris and is five years older than I am.

My mother's much younger sister Olga spent WW2 defending Moscow. Her son Dimitri lives there now. I have had very little contact with him.

Nina never wanted to visit Moscow because of bad memories. Her father Arthur was arrested by secret police at 3 AM one morning. They told her "go back to sleep young lady. We just want to talk to your father ". He was arrested because his brother lived in Germany and joined the Nazi party, when the two countries had a joint agreement of nonaggression.

Arthur died in the Gulags. His wife received a letter that he had died. The road to the Gulags is called the road of bones.

So Nina did not go back to Moscow for a long time. I also did not visit Moscow because I had top security clearance to work in weapons labs and at IIT on contracts such as how to shoot down missiles. Ala went to Moscow many times. She was too young to remember her father's arrest.

3

German Occupation of Ukraine

After the Germans occupied our experimental agricultural station we moved to a nearby town where my parents worked sorting seeds and ate in the employee cafeteria. I ate the food we had brought with us. It smelled of DDT because it had been sprayed in storage. When the Germans sent their own agricultural engineers to Ukraine, all the Ukrainian agricultural engineers were told to report to their former jobs. My father's job assignment was to send to Berlin the information of what was grown in Ukraine and how much. The officials in Berlin did not believe how much the Ukrainian soil produced so the Germans took only half the produce. Stalin always took 95%. Once my father worked for the Germans we had to leave with them because he had worked for the enemy. When the Germans started their slow retreat, the German secret police, Gestapo asked my father whether we are leaving with them.

4

Travel from Ukraine to a Camp and Germany

We left the agricultural experimental station in the summer of 1943 in a covered wagon. My mother's parents and grandmother came with us. We crossed the river Dnepr and stayed on the other side of the river until winter. My mother's family could not go with us further. The temperature was the coldest on record, -40 degrees Celsius one night. On their way home to Moscow my mother's father was killed in an automobile accident and my mother's grandmother fell ill and died. My mother's mother returned to Moscow alone to live with her daughter Olga.

Our trip in winter was first in a covered wagon, then by car and finally by train to a work camp, surrounded by wire. On the way a horse pulling our wagon kicked my father and broke his ribs. In the camp we slept in the barracks. For food we picked mushrooms to supplement the food my parents had in return for their labor in a factory. My mother knew which mushrooms were good to eat. A rabbit visited me through wires in our camp. My mother sold it to the Germans for a bag of potatoes. These Germans later had to flee because this territory was not part of Germany any more.

We traveled to Quedlinburg, Germany by train. Soon after this territory was given to the Russians in exchange for Berlin. My mother spoke English and convinced the occupying British to give us permission to go to Heidelberg, Headquarters of the American army. Heidelberg had one of the most famous and oldest universities in Europe, established in the 14th century. It was not destroyed in WW2. My uncle Vadim and my aunt Olga worked in the university after coming from Ukraine. There I met the first dark man. He later became the king of Thailand.

We lived with my uncle and aunt in a two bed room apartment. There was little food so my parents and I moved to a refugee camp in Mannheim . This city like most other German towns was nearly destroyed by bombs during the war. We had lots of food but the Russians visited the camp to convince us to go back to Russia. According to the Yalta treaty we were required to go back but the American general there said he never heard of such a treaty and we could stay if we wanted to. Nevertheless my parents were afraid and so we returned to Heidelberg.

My mother got a job with the American WACs and we rented an apartment in Rohrbacher Strasse.

We now had lots of food. Since my parents were working I ate lunch in German restaurants.

I often went hiking in the hills with Helene and her father. She was only six and did not remember this later.

5

German Schools and Christianity

In Heidelberg I took an exam in German to enter Realgymnasium which is like high school here. To improve my German my mother hired a tutor, Herr Reiser. He lost his leg during the war. He taught me how to write well. He *taught composition in my school and was probably the best teacher in the school. In history class we only studied the pre-Christian Germany. The Germans were* probably afraid to teach recent history under American occupation. For 3 years we studied arithmetic. Some of the problems were hard. Algebra would have made these problems easy. I learned this in Seward Park High School in New York City. On Saturdays I was an alter boy in the Russian Orthodox Church and I also took Sunday School classes.

Our distant uncle Grisha was a priest in New York City in the Ukrainian church. He helped us get visas to come to the USA. We waited 3 years. In the meantime President Truman created the Displaced Persons Act. It allowed us to come to the USA free of charge on a military boat that transported American troops during WW2.

6

Travel to New York City & Our Life There

We spent 3 years waiting for a visa to come to the USA. We finally came to the USA via the President Truman Displaced Persons Act aboard the ship General Muir. This ship was used to transport American troops to Europe during WW2. When we disembarked in New York City, my aunt Olga met us in a taxi and took us to her house on 14th Street. The rent was $20 per month. Later aunt Olga got a job at Columbia University with professor Dobjanski and her family moved to a university apartment. Dobjanski was a famous biologist. His funding came from the Atomic Energy Commission who were interested in mutations caused by radiation. When I was in college I worked in his lab and learned a lot of organic chemistry that helped me get an A in this difficult subject.

7

My Mother, Father and Me in New York

As an entomologist my mother could not find a job in her profession with pay. To make money she worked at night cleaning offices. In the daytime she volunteered at the American Museum of Natural History. She published 3 Bulletins with her own drawings:

1. North American Caterpillar Hunters of the Genera Calosoma and Callisthenes by Tatiana Gidaspow, Vol 116, article 3, New York.1959.

2. The Genus Calusoma in Central America, the Antilles and South America.Vol 124,Article 5,New York 1963 By Tatiana Gidaspow,Vol 124,Artilce 7, New York 1963.

3. A Revision of the Ground Beetles belonging to Saph 140, article 3,New York,1968.

My father worked in a Russian match factory.

For vacation we went to Miami Beach, Florida by bus. When the bus stopped in Virginia, I went to look for a bathroom. I stopped motionless when I saw the sign: White Only!

This sign was gone the next time we went to Florida.

Most weekends in the summer in New York we took the subway and then a bus to go to Pelham Bay. My mother and I were swimming. She remembered swimming in the Black Sea in Ukraine with the dolphins. My father fished and used to catch eels. They are very tasty when fresh. Later he went fishing at the end of Long Island in the Atlantic Ocean. He used to catch the biggest fish and win prizes. He cleaned the fish and my mother cooked it at home.

One time I went to Pelham Bay by myself. I saw some animal crossing my path. It stopped in front of me and I waved my bag at it. It sprayed some fluid into my eyes which burned. I ran to the water and cleaned my eyes. I took a bus to go home. Some passengers said there must be a skunk somewhere. In the train all passengers left my compartment.

On New Year's eve we went to see the Christmas show at Radio City Music Hall. During the rest of the year I went to many Broadway plays.

My father was a heavy smoker. He smoked Machorka whose seeds he brought with him from Ukraine. He grew it on our window sills.

8

High School, College and Beginning of Graduate School

I took a bus to go to Seward Park High School in New York. They taught German and therefore attracted a lot of students. My best friend was Stanley Engelsberg who later got a degree in physics from MIT and was a professor all his life.

I graduated from high school at the top of my class in 1952. I went to a tuition free college, the City College of New York.

The first year there I was picked by the registrar along with other top students to help students take their required courses. At CCNY the chemistry was good. Other required courses in engineering were good for passing the New York State exam to be a practicing engineer. But chemical engineering was poor, except for the unit operations lab developed by professor Schurig for whom I later worked at the Polytechnic Institute of Brooklyn. In the unit operations class the professor only talked about the stock market. Today unit operations involves conservation of mass, momentum and energy. No one in the department knew this subject. The bright students rebelled. As a punishment the Chairman of the department told the faculty to give the students grades no higher than C. Some ignored his advice. *But a newly hired faculty gave our Squad of 4 a C, after praising us as the best Squad he had.*

The grades were especially important then because men could be drafted and be sent to Korea if they had low grades in school. I graduated from CCNY cum laude in 1956.

In the summer I found an excellent job at Air Products, near Allentown, Pennsylvania. For one month there I worked on an urgent problem for their director of research. He was the smartest man I knew. This is why Air Products grew so big. My immediate supervisor was Lapin. He had obtained a Master's degree from Brooklyn Poly, with Schurig as his thesis advisor. He did not provide details about Schurig but urged me to stay at Air Products or go to graduate school elsewhere. I ignored his advice. At Brooklyn Poly I worked for Schurig in his unit operations lab. This experience was great for me. One of Schurig's former students warned me not to do a thesis under his direction but I did not listen to him either. My Master's thesis was his consulting job. The results of my experiments were not what the company wanted to see. Schurig never looked at my experiments.

I proved that my observations were correct. They are in my thesis, Arsenic-Aluminum-Zink Equilibrium, Dimitri Gidaspow, June 1959. My thesis was signed by Schurig and the head of the department, Othmer in 1958. A young professor, Naphtali told them that I deserve to get a PhD degree for this research. Othmer strongly recommended me to the Institute of Gas Technology for a work-study program that paid the students 2/3 of engineer's salary.

Brooklyn Poly in general treated their students very poorly. Brooklyn Poly became part of New York University, but with no professors from Brooklyn Poly, unfortunately not even Naphtali. Professor Othmer is best known for his book, the Kirk-Othmer encyclopedia. He became very rich from consulting in Japan and by investing his money wisely.

He left all his money to the American Chemical Society upon his death. AIChE did not treat him well. They never admitted him to their academy.

My best experience at Brooklyn Poly were the full-time graduate students. Often we went out for a beer together. Three of them were my groomsmen at our Russian orthodox wedding. Marvin Warshay came to our *Orthodox wedding in New York City from Chicago.* He worked at NASA in Cleveland all his life. We remained friends for a long time.

Our wedding in New York City with wedding party

PART

9

South Side Chicago,1958, Professor Ralph Peck and our Snorkling Trips.

I came to IIT's Gas Technology Institute (IGT) in August of 1958. To be admitted to the work-study-program you had to be a male US Citizen. The chairman of the department and my PhD thesis advisor Rex Ellington allowed the graduate students to work on their theses only. There were only 3 of us not from Chicago. I was the only one without a car. Since the food in the cafeteria was poor, I took a bus or walked to downtown, about 5 miles. One day on my way back home I was robbed. The police did nothing. When this almost happened again close to IGT, I considered leaving.

I stayed because I had a lot to learn from the chairman of chemical engineering, Ralph Peck, my future PhD thesis co-advisor. He was ahead of his time in teaching transport phenomena. Dr. Peck taught students how to think on their feet. He is remembered for his 10 minute quizzes.

Helene and I went snorkeling many times in Florida but two of our best snorkeling adventures were to Saint Croix in the Virgin Islands from a boat and in Puerto Rico near the shore on a tiny island.

10

Friends at IGT

At IGT I was friends with Magasanic who obtained his BS degree from McGill University in Montreal. He came to IGT with his wife who had worked as a model. In Canada he had learned how to pilot an airplane. He invited Helene and me to fly with them to New York during the winter in a small airplane that he rented. The trip to New York was fine, but on the way back we got into a storm and had a hard time finding an airport to land. I did not want to fly with them anymore.

At IGT I met Abbas Firoozabadi who after getting his PhD degree returned to teach in Iran. He invited me to give a short course at their university. The lecture hall was full when I talked about nuclear energy but nearly empty for my other 9 lectures. The young professors there talked to me about getting rid of the Shah. I had asked them who will rule Iran next. They had no idea. After Ayatollah Khomeini took over Abbas had to flee Iran despite the fact that he is the only devout Muslim I know. He is now a distinguished research professor of chemical engineering at Rice University in Houston. Two of his students took my CFD course online at IIT.

I met Charlie Solbrig when he was an undergraduate student in mechanical engineering and was assigned to help me take measurements. He lived with his wife Carol on the southside of Chicago. He married Carol before his graduation. They had 3 daughters and later a son. We often took a train and then a bus to their house. His father was a medical doctor who for a while owned the Solbrig Memorial Hospital in Chicago.

Once we went on a canoe trip with Charlie and Carol in the boundery lakes near Canada. We rented 2 canoes without motors that we had to carry on our shoulders from one lake to the next. We both fished but caught nothing. We ate only the food we brought with us.

We also drove to Florida together several times. One time we drove back to Chicago with stops for refueling only. We were all very tired and did not speak to each other.

Charlie worked at IITRI after getting his BS degree. He did his PhD part-time under my direction. It was an extension of my PhD thesis. My supervisor at IGT Bukachek made me rewrite my proposal for Charlie many times. With Charlie we published several papers jointly. After graduation Charlie joined IGT as an adjunct assistant professor. Our first joint student was Robert W. Lyczkowski who much later wrote a book, The History of Multiphase Science and Computational Fluid Dynamics, A Personal Memoir, Springer,2018. Charlie realized that IGT was not a good place to work. He left and found a job at the Atomic Energy commission in Idaho to work on the design of nuclear reactors. With Dan Hughes they developed a model for the design and obtained a lot of money from DOE. Charlie needed help with programming and went to Los Alamos. There W.C.Rivard and M.D.Torrey copied their model without permission: K-FIX, Jan 1979,US Dept

of Energy. Charlie wanted my opinion about the model. I went to Idaho on leave from IGT and with Bob found that the model was ill-posed as an initial value problem. See, Characteristics of unsteady one dimensional two phase flow, D. Gidaspow, R.W. Lyczkowski, C.W. Solbrig, E.D. Hughes and G.A. Mortensen, Trans. American Nuclear Society,17,249-250 (1973). Unfortunately DOE headquarters in Washington did not understand what ill—posedness was and blacklisted me. They told NSF not to give me any money. Fortunately Dr.Ojalvo at NSF knew me and did not listen to DOE. We had a large grant from the Solar Energy Institute in Colorado with professor Lavan from our mechanical engineering department. We wrote the proposal with his student, W.W. Worek while I was still at IGT who had an earlier contract from the gas industry. But their unit required a high temperature for regeneration and therefore could not be regenerated with low level solar energy. Our design was based on the PhD thesis of Roy Dipak, Nonlinear coupled heat and mass exchange in a cross-flow regenerator, R.Dipak and D.Gidaspow, Chemical Engineering Science 29,2101-2114 (1974). DOE funded our proposal for 3 years. I went with Lavan to Colorado every 3 months to present our progress. I went skiing with him in Colorado and in California. Lavan liked to ski until the slopes closed. One time it snowed and the cars needed chains but our rented car did not have them. We slid down the big mountain and I thought we would slide off the road.

I went skiing when I worked with Charlie in Idaho on nearby hills. Once I went skiing with Charlie, his wife and his 3 daughters in Montana. I could ski only with their youngest daughter. The others were too advanced for me.

In Chicago Helene and I took our son skiing when he was 3 years old. By the time he was five he could ski and really liked it. One of his favorite places to go was the Playboy Club in Lake Geneva Wisconsin, where the waitresses were dressed as bunnies. Misha liked them and they liked him. We often went to ski in Alpine Valley in Wisconsin. Later we also drove with him to Indian Head, Michigan, a day of driving from our house. There they had girls take off their coats and ski in bikinis. Our friend Charles Wittmann who at that time was assistant professor at IIT went skiing with us several times. Once one of the girls serving us in a bar told Charles " Take me back home in your suitcase ". Charles went to see her later. She had a huge boyfriend in the bar with her.

Charles came to visit us in Northbrook many times after getting a job in industry. The last time I went skiing was with Alex Nikolov who came to meet me at our house early in the morning. We went to Alpine Valley. On the way to the top in the lift my right ski came off. When getting of the lift I fell down and nearly broke my right arm. I had my arm in a sling for 6 months. This was the last time I skiied.

At IGT I met George Buzyna who worked for my advisor Rex Ellington doing his MS thesis. George, his brother Lenny and his parents came to the USA from Western Ukraine. He did his PhD thesis on the East Coast and later went to work at the Florida State University in Tallahassee. We went to visit them many times. To retire early George received two times his salary for 5 years. He bought a boat. We went out on their boat with them several times. We also flew to Tallahassee for their 50th wedding anniversary celebration. Lenny Buzyna and his wife Nina lived just north of us in Deerfield. We enjoyed many Ravinia concerts with them. Unfortunately Lenny died suddenly during the pandemic of a heart attack.

The best part of IGT for me was my work with Bernie Baker who was in charge of a large fuel cell project. We obtained a grant from DOE to improve the fuel cells needed for moon travel. Based on this work Bernie Baker, Bob Lyczkowski and I received a certificate of merit from Dr. Werner von Braun in September 1970. This was Bob's MS thesis. I was also a co-advisor of Baker's PhD thesis with Wasan. He used the method of

Green's functions to improve fuel cells. He sent me to give a talk in Japan in 1966 and then travel around the world to give lectures in Paris and Switzerland. Bernie left IGT and founded his own company that employed many of my students. Once Bernie left IGT it was time for me leave also. Because of our work on the moon program I was invited to Houston to witness the return of the astronauts from the moon.

Santiago Chuck worked for Baker and me on an IGT fuel cell project. His mother visited him in Chicago from Mexico and invited Helene and me for lunch. She made the best tamales I ever had. After obtaining his Master's degree Santiago went to teach at the Monterrey University and became dean of engineering soon after. He invited me to give a talk at their university. It was winter in Chicago and also cold in Monterrey and therefore his wife suggested I should visit the famous Mexican resort Acapulco for a few days before my lecture. When I arrived in Acapulco it felt like heaven. Unfortunately the hotel was up on a hill and the taxis were hard to find because this was the time of the year when many Mexicans visited Acapulco. I wanted to go snorkeling but because of miscommunication I went scuba diving instead which I had never done before. I was only able to float until one of the boat attendants attached a weight to me which enabled me to dive very well. Soon I ran out of air and almost drowned before they realized that I was in trouble and came to my rescue. At night in my hotel room I woke up and only then realized why I almost drowned. It was the added weight!

Frank Kulacki obtained his BS degree in mechanical engineering at IIT in 1963 and joined IGT after his graduation. He did his MS thesis under my direction. It was an extension of my PhD thesis. After getting his PhD degree from the University of Minnesota Frank went to teach at Ohio State University. He was very successful in getting grants. I took an interview there to become director of research because I was considering leaving IGT.

Frank was dean of engineering for most of his career. His Google scholar h index is 41, which is a very high rating. We attended an international engineering meeting in Japan, where we tried to explain the meaning of ill-posedness. Before the meeting we visited Hokeido, where the Olympics were held the year before.

11

My advisors Rex Ellington, Ralph Peck and Me.

The gas industry was interested in eliminating nitric oxide during combustion. Rex Ellington had such a project at IGT but the device they built kept breaking. To withstand high temperatures it was made of vitreous alumina. When I came to IGT I rebuilt the equipment, including a moving probe to measure concentrations. I used hydrogen as the fuel and coated the alumina surface with platinum to obtain reactions at low temperatures. In 1960 I measured the wall temperature. It increased sharply from 200 to 600 degrees F and then rose to 1600 degrees F. The highest rate of reaction was 6 lbmoles/hr sq ft atm.

I developed a theory to explain the results that were presented by Rex Ellington at the Fuels Division of ASME meeting in California in 1961. The name of our paper is Heat Transfer in an Infinite Tube supporting surface combustion. It is attached in 11 pictures. At the meeting instead of presenting my measurements Rex talked about applications only. The chairman complained about this but still invited us to publish our paper. I made a mistake not publishing our paper. I did not put these results into my PhD Thesis because professor Swanson who was on my committee said you were not allowed to include published information in a thesis. This is the reverse of what American universities were doing. He did the same to my students later on.

My PhD thesis, Surface Combustion of Hydrogen, June 1962 was published in two parts in the AIChE Journal.

Close to the end of my experimental study Ellington asked Dr. Peck, who soon was leaving for a year-long sabbatical in Israel, to be my co-advisor. He asked me to teach his graduate course in heat transfer and thermodynamics. Swanson, the acting chairman, asked me to also teach other undergraduate courses without additional compensation. I never worked so hard in my life.

Since I was not interested in teaching then I interviewed at the central research labs of DuPont. At that time DuPont's chemistry was the best in the world. Now they do not exist anymore because the last CEO did not want to see any "moon programs ". From du Pont I obtained several offers with excellent pay. When Rex found this out, he asked me to come back to IGT as an assistant professor. Since I still could be drafted and sent to Vietnam and was promised to have a PhD student work with me, I accepted the offer from Rex.

The best part of IGT was its excellent students. My first PhD student was Charles Solbrig, whose father owned the Solbrig Memorial hospital. With Solbrig we taught the first course in computational techniques. My friend Robert W. Lyczkowski in his personal memoir, the history of multiphase science and computational fluid dynamics, Springer (2018) describes what we worked on and how it was received.

IGT worked on several important problems: fuel cells and solar air conditioning. I worked on fuel cells with

Bernie Baker, with funding from the space program. The director of IGT was Henry Linden. I helped him with a Russian delegation who came to us for assistance to buy pipelines for pumping natural gas from Siberia to Europe. Our military did not allow us to sell this to the Russians. In the end the West Germans sold them the pipelines.

I obtained good advice from Linden but his assistant from industry with only BS degrees did not like me and gave me a hard time. Therefore I had to leave IGT. I had several potential offers to be a director of research. Darsh Wasan, the chairman of chemical engineering offered me the du Pont salary which I accepted. We got to know Darsh and his wife Usha well and enjoyed many good times together. We also attended their 50th wedding anniversary celebration.

Lavan from mechanical engineering and I obtained the largest funding IIT had until that time for a desiccant solar air conditioning project. President Carter supported this program, but no other president since him.

PAPER NUMBER 61-SA-59

Heat Transfer in an Infinite Tube-Supporting Surface Combustion

D. GIDASPOW

PhD Candidate,
Institute of Gas
Technology,
Chicago, III.

R. T. ELLINGTON

Assistant Research Director,
Chairman, Education Program,
Institute of Gas Technology,
Chicago, III.

Most efforts to describe surface combustion have been qualitative in nature; the quantitative efforts have frequently involved gross assumption regarding system behavior without proper justification. In this paper, a set of equations for one-dimensional change is solved for a constant-pressure process to describe surface combustion in an infinite tube. The reaction rate constant is approximated by a step function of surface temperature. Experimental results are presented to show the validity of the assumption. Experimental reaction rate data for isothermal surface combustion of hydrogen in air in turbulent flow were obtained for a platinum-coated vitreous alumina tube between 200 and 1600 F. The rate of reaction was found as a function of hydrogen concentration and surface temperature. Heat-transfer coefficients with surface combustion were compared with measured coefficients for pure air and agreed closely for the case considered.

Contributed by the Fuels Division for presentation at the Summer Annual Meeting, Los Angeles, Calif., June 11-15, 1961, of The American Society of Mechanical Engineers. Manuscript received at ASME Headquarters, April 21, 1961.

Written discussion on this paper will be accepted up to July 17, 1961.

Copies will be available until April 1, 1962.

Heat Transfer in an Infinite Tube-Supporting Surface Combustion

D. GIDASPOW

R. T. ELLINGTON

NOMENCLATURE

A = cross-sectional area of tube, sq ft

a = defined by equation (22)

b = defined by equation (23)

c_p = heat capacity at constant pressure, Btu/lb-deg F

C_1, C_2, C_1, C_2 = integration constants in section with and without reaction, respectively

G = mass rate of flow per unit cross-sectional area of tube, lb/hr-sq ft

h = heat-transfer coefficient, Btu/hr-sq ft-deg F

K_c = first-order reaction rate constant for surface reactions, lb moles 1/hr-sq ft-atm

k = thermal conductivity of tube along its length, Btu/hr-ft-deg F

L = length of tube

M_1 = molecular weight of species 1, $\left(\dfrac{\text{lb } 1}{\text{lb mole } 1}\right)$

M_{mo} = mean molecular weight of feed, $\left(\dfrac{\text{lb feed}}{\text{lb mole feed}}\right)$

n = moles of species 1 per mole of feed

n_o = moles of species 1 entering per mole of feed, or mole fraction of 1 in feed

n_t = total number of moles in system at any time per mole of feed

P_t = total pressure, atm

R = inside tube radius, ft

R' = outside tube radius, ft

r = net molar rate of consumption of species 1 per unit surface area by chemical reaction (lb moles 1/hr-sq ft) surface

r' = net molar rate of consumption of species 1 per unit reactor volume by chemical reaction, lb moles 1/hr-cu ft

r'' = net molar rate of consumption of species 1 per unit volume of solid conducting tube by chemical reaction, lb moles 1/hr-cu ft solid tube

S = surface area of tube, sq ft

T = surface temperature in section with reaction, deg F

T' = surface temperature in section without reaction, deg F

t = gas temperature in section with reaction, deg F

t' = gas temperature in section without reaction, deg F

V = volume of tube, cu ft

v = linear velocity of gas, fph

Y_1 = weight fraction of species 1, lb 1/lb mixture

y = mole fraction of species 1, lb moles 1/lb mole mixture

α = defined by equation (24)

β = defined by equation (25)

δ = tube thickness for narrow tubes or in general $= (R'^2-R^2)/2R$

ρ = density of gas, pcf

τ = time, hr

ΔH = heat of reaction at constant pressure and operating temperature defined to be positive for exothermic reactions, Btu/lb mole species 1

Subscripts

C = chemical

1 = referring to species 1

ig = ignition

in = inlet

max = maximum

mo = referring to mean value of feed

o = at position zero

p = at constant pressure P

t = total

INTRODUCTION

Research on surface combustion started in 1817 when Sir Humphry Davy (1)[1] discovered that a warm spiral of platinum wire brought about the ignition of hydrogen. Later investigators, such as Dulong and Thenard, William Henry, Graham, Faraday, Mendeleev, and De la Rive studied the accelerating effect of surfaces on the combustion of hydrogen. Bodenstein (2) attempted the experimental measurement of reaction velocities, the complexity of the phenomena soon became apparent from his work. In 1906, Bone and Wheeler (3) published work dealing with applications (4). A great deal of development along practical lines took place in the Soviet Union following World War II; this was summarized by Ravich (5). The Soviet experimental work was apparently oriented

---

[1] Underlined numbers in parentheses designate References at the end of the paper.

toward study of catalysts. No rate constants or activation energies are given, so the data can be compared only semi-quantitatively. Since the model presented in this paper is based on experimental rate data for combustion of hydrogen, the reviews by Emmett (6) and in "Advances in Catalysis" (7) are important. However, the reaction data in these references are generally for low temperatures and are not in terms of rate constants. The data must be examined in detail to discern a general trend.

In the last fifteen years several more mathematical papers have appeared. Frank-Kamenetskii (8) discussed ignition and extinction for first-order Arrhenius-behavior reactions, but restricts his results by neglecting conduction in the solid and heat absorption of the gas. Chukhanov has published several papers on surface combustion (9-13). One of these (13) bears directly on the analysis made in this paper and gives a qualitative description of the process. However, in developing his basic rate equation he employs linear velocity rather than mass velocity. Later, he multiplies the ratio of mass-transfer coefficient to linear velocity by the ratio of surface temperature to gas temperature, to correct for nonisothermal conditions. Comparison with common mass-transfer correlations leads to a different conclusion. On the basis of his analysis, Chukhanov concludes that, when diffusion controls, the ceramic tube will have a uniform temperature along the entire length of the tube. In view of the analysis presented in this paper, one must question this conclusion.

A 1954 paper on simultaneous heat and mass transfer in tubular reactors by Satterfield, et al (14) gives only a rough analysis of surface temperature produced by reaction. A 1958 paper (15) on migration of ignition zones by Wicke and Vortmeyer, does not attempt to treat this more difficult problem from the point of view of conservation equations. Data for homogeneous-heterogeneous combustion of carbon monoxide in narrow tubes are presented by Khitrin and Solovyeva (16). They believe the process can be divided into reaction on the surface and in the bulk or homogeneous phase. The associated heat-transfer problem is not discussed. Heat transfer in porous media has been discussed in considerable detail in connection with porous-wall cooling, but not extensively in regard to reacting systems.

The process of surface combustion has long been important in industrial heat processing. The general lack of reaction data for the process has prevented mathematical representation of its behavior. This has often prevented optimum design of combustion equipment and resulted in the practical difficulties of burner flashback and localized overheating with refractory melting. Modern problems of significant importance are the complete oxidation of a gaseous fuel at low temperatures and the behavior of porous-media combustors in a variety of environments under both steady and unsteady-state conditions.

The capillary-bundle model is frequently employed in efforts to describe the behavior of packed beds and porous media. This results in idealizing the behavior of each tube because radial losses are eliminated. As a start toward describing the behavior of real systems, the authors present analytic discussion of the behavior of a single tube with a heterogeneous reaction on its inner surface, and the temperature profiles resulting from given system parameters. Development of relations yielding these profiles must include terms involving the rate of the surface reaction. Since adequate rate data are not available in the literature, the authors utilize rate information obtained experimentally in study of the fundamentals of the surface combustion of hydrogen with air, which is being conducted at IGT.

EXPERIMENTAL METHOD AND RATE LAW

Although this paper is primarily analytical in nature, experimental reaction-rate information is used in the development. A brief review of the method of obtaining the rate data and the experimental results will be presented to show their applicability to this problem. A detailed discussion of observed reaction behavior will be presented elsewhere when current work is completed.

Combustion of hydrogen on the surface of a platinum-coated vitreous alumina tube was studied between 200 and 1600 F. One-tenth to three per cent hydrogen mixtures flowed at Reynolds numbers between roughly 10,000 and 60,000 through a 1/2-in. tubular reactor and were allowed to burn on the tube surface. The surface was maintained at constant temperature by means of eight heating elements with adjustable power inputs arranged along the tube. Homogeneous reaction was suppressed by using cold air feed and dilute mixtures. Data for portions of the tube for which substantial reaction occurred in the boundary layer are not included in this discussion. The surface temperature was measured by means of eight thermocouples deeply imbedded in the tube. Heat fluxes were such that the difference between the actual and indicated tube-wall temperature was less than 15 deg F in all cases. Hydrogen-air samples were taken at several positions along

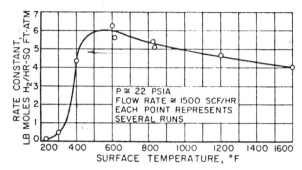

Fig. 1 Effect of surface temperature on hydrogen oxidation reaction rate

TABLE 1 REACTION RATE CONSTANTS, HYDROGEN-AIR
(Average values, disregarding entrance and exit sections)

Surface Temp = 601°F, Feed Rate = 1475 ±10 SCFH

Run No.	49	50	51	52	53	54
Inlet H_2, %	1.445	0.976	0.630	0.476	0.268	0.122
Exit H_2, %	0.952	0.668	0.417	0.308	0.178	0.077
Avg.	1.199	0.822	0.524	0.392	0.223	0.100
$K_c(\frac{lb\ mole}{sq\ ft/hr/atm})$	6.40	5.81	6.29	6.64	6.30	7.02

Surface Temp = 1200°F, Feed Rate = 1481 ±20 SCFH

Run No.	56	57	58	59	60	61
Inlet H_2, %	2.99	2.51	1.857	1.300	0.756	0.311
Exit H_2, %	2.17	1.81	1.313	0.919	0.542	0.453
Avg.	2.58	2.16	1.585	1.110	0.649	0.382
$K_c(\frac{lb\ mole}{sq\ ft/hr/atm})$	4.43	4.65	4.80	4.82	4.61	5.26

the tube by means of a water-cooled probe provided with a high-velocity thermocouple to measure gas-stream temperatures. Samples were taken beyond the thermal and mass-transfer entrance regions. Continuous hydrogen analysis was obtained by use of a thermal-conductivity analyzer.

The rate of reaction was found as a function of hydrogen concentration and surface temperature. At high flow rates, the rate of reaction was essentially independent of flow rate. Therefore, it was concluded that in this region the rate of reaction was not affected appreciably by film diffusion, but was controlled by chemical-reaction rate. In this "chemically" controlled region, the rate was found to be proportional to the mole fraction of hydrogen in the stream. Assuming linear variation with total pressure over a narrow pressure range, the rate constant (lb moles H_2 reacted per hr per sq ft surface per atm) was calculated. The extent of the independence of the first-order rate constant of mole fraction of hydrogen is shown in Table 1. The rate constant was found to increase exponentially with temperature up to roughly 450 F and then to level off and decrease slightly with temperature to 1600 F, Fig. 1. The activation energies for the two regions are 17 and 0.66 kilocalories per gram-mole, respectively. A mechanism tentatively assigned to the controlling process in the high-temperature region is the rate of adsorption of hydrogen. The defense of this hypothesis will be deferred until more information is available on rates for this surface and the others being studied.

The behavior in Fig. 1 can be interpreted as follows: The rate of reaction increases rapidly with temperature over a narrow range and then levels off to become relatively independent of temperature. For analysis of energy balances in flowing systems, the small amount of heat liberated, below the critical temperature of rate

increase, is overshadowed by other effects and may be neglected.

The change in mechanism of the reaction above the critical range may be due to control by diffusion, adsorption, or other processes. If the rate of diffusion to the reactor surface controls, as often happens, the rate will increase proportionally to the roughly 0.15 power of temperature, as seen from the common mass-transfer correlations. There is the further possibility of decrease in catalytic activity with increase in catalyst temperature. Thus, the rate is effectively independent of temperature. The data presented in Fig. 1 show a reaction whose rate slowly decreases with surface temperature beyond a fixed temperature. This rate can be approximated by a step function, and such a representation is used in our analysis.

KINETICS IN A FLOW SYSTEM

The continuity equations of total mass and species 1 for mono-directional flow are:

$$\frac{\partial \rho}{\partial \tau} + \frac{\partial (\rho v)}{\partial L} = 0 \tag{1}$$

$$\frac{\partial (\rho Y_1)}{\partial \tau} + \frac{\partial (\rho v Y_1)}{\partial L} = -r_1' M_1 \tag{2}$$

These equations can be applied to laminar flow, and to turbulent flow by use of properly averaged quantities. In this case, turbulent fluctuations in composition and axial diffusion must be regarded as negligibly small. For steady state,

$$\frac{\partial (\rho v)}{\partial L} = 0 \tag{3}$$

$$Y_1 \frac{\partial (\rho v)}{\partial L} + (\rho v) \frac{\partial Y_1}{\partial L} = -r_1' M_1 \tag{4}$$

Substituting equation (3) into (4) yields:

$$(\rho v) \frac{dY_1}{dL} = -r_1' M_1 \qquad (5)$$

For surface reactions, the over-all rate of reaction is proportional to the active surface area. For two-dimensional systems, the rate would appear as a boundary condition for the equations describing the change. In this case, however, the rate is inserted in equation (5) directly. The basis of equation (5) can be changed by use of equation (6), which equates the rate of disappearance of a given species for a given increment of reactor length, based on the surface area, to the rate of disappearance based on the reactor volume for the same incremental length of reactor

$$r' \Delta V = r \Delta S \qquad (6)$$

The conversion will hold for plug flow or flow with fully established concentration profiles and relatively small concentration changes. With this modification the defining rate equation becomes

$$(\rho v) \frac{dY_1}{dL} = - \left(\frac{S}{V}\right) r_1 M_1 \qquad (7)$$

Multiplying through by the cross-sectional area yields

$$\left(\frac{GA}{M_1}\right) dY_1 = - \frac{2\pi R \Delta L}{\pi R^2 \Delta L} (\pi R^2 r_1 dL) = -r_1 dS \qquad (8)$$

If n-moles of species 1 are reacted per mole of feed, of initial mole fraction n_o and a mean molecular weight M_{mo}, the weight fraction at any time is given by

$$Y_1 = \frac{(n_o-n) M_1}{M_{mo}} \qquad (9)$$

Equation (8) then becomes a definition of reaction rate

$$\left(\frac{GA}{M_{mo}}\right) dn = r_1 dS \qquad (10)$$

The mole fraction of species 1, is given by

$$y = \frac{n_o-n}{n_t} \qquad (11)$$

where n_t is the total number of moles per mole of feed. For small changes in total moles with reaction, this quantity approaches unity. Furthermore, if the rate law is given by

$$r = K_c P_t y \qquad (12)$$

integration of equation (10) gives

$$- \ln (y/y_o) = \frac{K_c P_t M_{mo} S}{GA} \qquad (13)$$

This equation was used to calculate the rate constant shown in Fig.1. The same expression is obtained for the mass-transfer coefficient for complete diffusion control.

For a thin insulated tube of thickness δ and inside radius R, it is immaterial whether the heat is liberated by chemical reaction at the inner surface or throughout the bulk of the tube wall, and a new rate can be defined by

$$r'' = \frac{2\pi R \Delta L r}{[(R+\delta)^2 - R^2]\pi \Delta L} = \frac{r}{\delta} \qquad (14)$$

as δ becomes small.

The assumptions are that all chemical energy goes into heating the tube before being transferred elsewhere (substantiated experimentally by comparing heat-transfer coefficients with and without reaction) and that the radial temperature distribution can be neglected. With these assumptions the rate can be given by

$$r'' = \frac{K_c P_t y_o}{\delta} \exp\left(- \frac{2 K_c P_t M_{mo} L}{GR}\right) \qquad (15)$$

For the case when $\delta \ll R$ is not true, but the essential assumptions hold, a proper δ' can be calculated. In general

$$\delta' = \frac{(R+\delta)^2 - R^2}{2R}$$

ENERGY EQUATIONS FOR SURFACE REACTION IN A TUBE

Two energy equations are needed to describe the heat-transfer process accompanying surface combustion in a tube. One describes the energy transfer in the gas. The other relates the energy changes in the solid. For the gas phase, three more equations of change are in general needed to describe the process. The over-all continuity equation and the continuity equation for the reacting species have been used in describing the kinetics of the system. The momentum equation drops out under assumption of constant pressure. Viscous dissipation and conduction through the gas are also neglected.

Assume the gas is heated by convection and that any heating by radiation is included in the heat-transfer coefficient for convection. Then, at steady state, the energy equation of change for the element shown in Fig.2 is

$$\rho v c_p \frac{dt}{dL} (\pi R^2 dL) = h(T-t)(2\pi R dL) \qquad (16)$$

Simplifying equation (16), one obtains the energy equation for the gas

$$\frac{dt}{dL} = \frac{2h}{Gc_p R} (T-t) \qquad (17)$$

Assuming the chemical reaction takes place

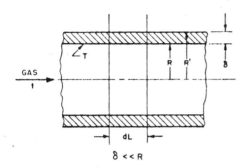

Fig. 2 Differential element of tube for energy
and material balance

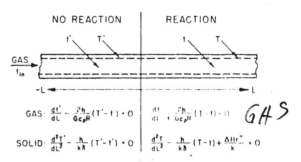

Fig. 3 Energy relationships of temperature profiles in
tube with active and inactive sections

on or in the solid, the energy equation for the
solid is

$$k \frac{d^2 T}{dx^2} (2\pi R \delta dL) - h(T-t)(2\pi R dL) \qquad (18)$$
$$+ r'' \Delta H (2\pi R \delta dL) = 0$$

For convenience, the heat of reaction was
considered positive for exothermic reactions.
Simplifying equation (18), one obtains the energy
equation for the solid

$$\frac{d^2 T}{dL^2} - \frac{h}{k\delta} (T-t) + \frac{\Delta H r''}{k} = 0 \qquad (19)$$

Assuming the physical properties and transfer
coefficients are calculated at the mean temperatures in question, it is possible to solve these
equations. Differentiating equation (17) and
adding to equation (19),

$$\frac{d^2 T}{dL^2} - \frac{d^2 t}{dL^2} + \frac{2h}{Gc_p R} \left[\frac{dT}{dL} - \frac{dt}{dL} \right]$$
$$\qquad\qquad\qquad\qquad\qquad (20)$$
$$- \frac{h}{k\delta} (T-t) + \frac{\Delta H r''}{k} = 0$$

This is a second-order linear differential equation in (T-t) with constant coefficients and a
nonhomogeneous term requiring a particular solution. The general solution of the complete equation, for the case of a first-order chemical reaction whose rate is given by equation (15), is

$$T-t = C_1 \exp(-aL + L\sqrt{a^2+b}) \qquad (21)$$
$$+ C_2 \exp(-aL - \sqrt{a^2+b}\ L) + \beta e^{-\alpha L}$$

where

$$a = h/Gc_p R \qquad (22)$$

$$b = h/k\delta \qquad (23)$$

$$\alpha = 2K_c P_t M_{mo}/GR \qquad (24)$$

$$\beta = \frac{\Delta H K_c P_t y_o}{k\delta(b + 2a\alpha - \alpha^2)} \qquad (25)$$

and $a > 0$, $b > 0$, $\alpha \geq 0$, $\beta \geq 0$.

SOLUTION FOR AN INFINITE TUBE

Consider two semi-infinite tubes, joined at
$L = 0$, having the same thermal conductivity and
dimensions, Fig. 3. Assume there is no reaction
on the tube surface on the left. Therefore K_c
in equation (15) and thus α and β in equation
(21) are zero for this portion of the tube. The
reaction starts at $L = 0$ and occurs on the tube
surface to the right. Physically, this may mean
that a long tube is coated from a certain point
on with a catalytic material which promotes the
surface reaction. Practically, the tube on the
left need not be long. Let primes refer to temperatures and integration constants for the tube
on the left. Excluding the source term, the energy equations previously developed apply for the
tube on the left.

A set of four ordinary linear differential
equations, two second-order and two first-order,
is to be solved simultaneously. The six boundary
conditions are as follows:
1 At $L \rightarrow \infty$, (T-t) must exist
2 At $L \rightarrow -\infty$, (T'-t') must exist and is
   zero. $t' = t_{in}$
3 and 4 At $L = 0$, $t = t'$ and $T = T'$, since
   the temperature distribution is continuous. At this position call $t = t_o$
   and $T = T_o$
5 and 6 At $L = 0$, $\frac{dt}{DL} = \frac{dt'}{dL}$ and $\frac{dT}{dL} = \frac{dT'}{dL}$
   since there is no source concentrated
   at $L = 0$

From boundary condition 1, C_1 in equation
(21) becomes zero, since $\sqrt{a^2+b} > a > 0$, except for

a trivial case. For the tube on the left in Fig. 3,

$$T'-t' = C_1' \exp(-aL + \sqrt{a^2+bL})$$
$$+ C_2' \exp(-aL - \sqrt{a^2+bL}) \qquad (26)$$

From boundary condition 2), $C_2' = 0$ in the above equation. From boundary conditions 3 and 4,

$$C_2 + \beta = C_1' \qquad (27)$$

Applying boundary conditions 5 and 6 to equations (21) and (26),

$$-C_2(a+\sqrt{a^2+b}) - \alpha\beta = C_1'(-a+\sqrt{a^2+b}) \qquad (28)$$

Solving for C_1' and C_2 and substituting into equation (21) remembering that C_1 was zero, gives

$$T-t = \beta\left[e^{-\alpha L} - \frac{\alpha-a+\sqrt{a^2+b}}{2\sqrt{a^2+b}} e^{-aL-\sqrt{a^2+b}\,L}\right] \qquad (29)$$

where

$$\frac{\alpha-a+\sqrt{a^2+b}}{2\sqrt{a^2+b}} > 0$$

Substituting the expression for (T-t) in equation (29) into equation (17) and integrating, using boundary condition 3, yields an expression for the gas temperature, t, in the reactive section in terms of t_o. To obtain t_o in terms of the incoming gas temperature t_{in}, the energy equation for the gas in the unheated section is integrated. The resulting expression for the gas temperature is as follows:

$$t = t_{in} + \frac{2a\beta}{\alpha} + \frac{2a\beta(2a-\alpha)}{b}$$
$$+ \frac{a\beta(\alpha-a+\sqrt{a^2+b})}{\sqrt{a^2+b}(a+\sqrt{a^2+b})}\exp(-aL-L\sqrt{a^2+b})$$
$$- \frac{2a\beta}{\alpha}\exp(-\alpha L) \qquad (30)$$

Combining this with the expression for (T-t), equation (29), the final expression for the surface temperature is obtained

$$T = t_{in} + \frac{2a\beta}{\alpha} + \frac{2a\beta(2a-\alpha)}{b} + \beta(1-\frac{2a}{\alpha})\exp(-\alpha L) +$$
$$\frac{\beta(\alpha-a+\sqrt{a^2+b})}{\sqrt{a^2+b}}\left[\frac{a}{a+\sqrt{a^2+b}} - \frac{1}{2}\right]\exp(-aL-L\sqrt{a^2+b}) \qquad (31)$$

where

$$\frac{2a\beta}{\alpha} + \frac{2a\beta(2a-\alpha)}{b} = \frac{\Delta H y_o}{c_p M_{mo}} \qquad (31a)$$

ANALYSIS OF SURFACE-TEMPERATURE PROFILES

Analysis of the expression for surface temperature reveals a number of interesting proper-

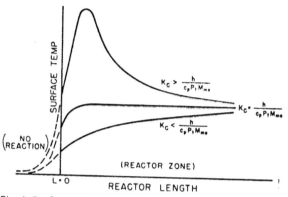

Fig. 4 Predicted temperature profiles of reaction conditions

ties. Differentiating equation (31) with respect to length, and setting the derivative equal to zero, one obtains the length at which the maximum temperature occurs

$$L_{max,T}$$
$$= \frac{1}{(\alpha-a-\sqrt{a^2+b})} \ln \frac{2(2a-\alpha)\sqrt{a^2+b}}{(\alpha-a+\sqrt{a^2+b})(a-\sqrt{a^2+b})} \qquad (32)$$

For a maximum to exist $\alpha > 2a$. This implies that $K_c > h/c_p P_t M_{mo}$ if a maximum surface temperature is to exist in $0 < L < \infty$. Taking the second derivative of T,

$$\frac{d^2T}{dL^2} = -\beta\alpha(2a-\alpha)e^{-\alpha L}$$
$$- \frac{\beta b(\alpha-a+\sqrt{a^2+b})}{2\sqrt{a^2+b}}\exp(-aL-L\sqrt{a^2+b}) \qquad (33)$$

The coefficient of the second exponential term always remains positive. For $\alpha < 2a$, the first coefficient is also positive. Therefore, for such a case the second derivative will always be negative. It approaches zero as L approaches infinity. The inflection point for $\alpha > 2a$ occurs at

$$L_{infl} = \frac{1}{(\alpha-a-\sqrt{a^2+b})} \ln\left[\frac{2\alpha(\alpha-2a)\sqrt{a^2+b}}{b(\alpha-a+\sqrt{a^2+b})}\right] \qquad (34)$$

(T-t) always becomes maximum at

$$L_{max(T-t)}$$
$$= \frac{1}{(\alpha-a-\sqrt{a^2+b})} \ln\left[\frac{(a+\sqrt{a^2+b})(\alpha-a+\sqrt{a^2+b})}{2\alpha\sqrt{a^2+b}}\right] \qquad (35)$$

Thus, temperature profiles with and without maxima are possible, Fig. 4. Several possible behaviors should be pointed out before detailed proof of them. System thermodynamics, equation (39), define the temperature asymptote, if reaction is initiated. The upper curve represents the case $\alpha > 2a$ and shows a temperature maximum downstream of the ignition point. The decay of the curve is controlled by the first derivative of equation (31). If the decay goes below T_{ig}, the reaction will be quenched. If $T_{L=0} < T_{ig}$ and the system parameters are such as to yield the lower curves, Fig.4, reaction will not start and the curves will not exist. If $T_{L=0} > T_{ig}$, the curves will exist and increase to the asymptotic value.

If the reaction rate constant is given by a step function $K_c = K_c$ for $T \geq T_{ig}$ and $K = 0$ for $T < T_{ig}$, then a criterion for spontaneous combustion at a steady state can be given. The experimentally determined rate constant can be approximated by such a function, as can diffusion-controlled reactions. On this basis it also makes sense to speak of a surface-ignition temperature, T_{ig}. For such cases the criterion for combustion on the surface without any external heat input or loss is:

$$\left[t_{in} + \frac{2a\beta(2a-\alpha)}{b} + \beta \right.$$
$$\left. + \frac{\beta(\alpha-a+\sqrt{a^2+b})}{\sqrt{a^2+b}} \left(\frac{a}{a+\sqrt{a^2+b}} - \frac{1}{2} \right) \right] \geq T_{ig} \quad (36)$$

This is seen from expression (31), remembering that reaction must occur as L approaches zero from the right. Should the temperature fall below T_{ig} anywhere, the reaction will effectively stop. For the important case of $b \gg a$ and $b \gg \alpha$, the criterion reduces to the following simple expression:

$$\left[t_{in} + \frac{\Delta H \, K_c P_t y_o}{2h} \right] \geq T_{ig} \quad (37)$$

The factor 2 in the denominator in equation (37) comes from the importance of conduction even when the heat transfer by this means is small compared to other modes. The same approximate expression will hold for a zero order chemical reaction, with $K_c P_t y_o$ in expression (37) replaced by the constant rate r_c.

At $L \to \infty$ the surface temperature becomes:

$$T_{L=\infty} = t_{in} + \frac{\Delta H y_o}{c_p M_{mo}} \quad (38)$$

Similarly the gas temperature, from equation (30), becomes,

$$t_{L=\infty} = t_{in} + \frac{\Delta H y_o}{c_p M_{mo}} \quad (39)$$

which, of course, is an ordinary adiabatic heat

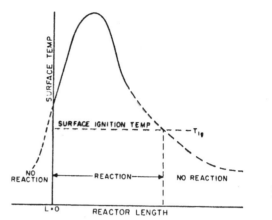

Fig. 5 Temperature profiles for reaction quenching $(K_c > 2h/c_p P_t M_{mo}$ and $T_{L=\infty} < T_{ig} T_{L=0})$

balance,

$$c_p(t_{L=\infty} - t_{in}) = \frac{\Delta H y_o}{M_{mo}} \quad (40)$$

For the case of $b \gg a$ and $b \gg \alpha$, comparing the reduced forms of expressions (36) and (38) it can be seen that $T_{L=\infty} < T_{L=0}$ implies

$$\frac{2a\beta}{\alpha} < \frac{1}{2}\beta \quad \text{or} \quad \alpha > 4a$$

Conversely $\alpha > 4a$ implies $T_{L=\infty} < T_{L=0}$. If $\alpha > 4a$ and $T_{L=\infty} < T_{ig} < T_{L=0}$, reaction can never go to completion in an adiabatic tube, no matter how long it is made. The same should apply to a porous burner or reactor of a composite configuration for the conditions specified. This is illustrated in Fig.5, neglecting the small distortion due to heat loss by conduction once reaction stops. Knowing the heat-transfer coefficients and the reaction-rate data, the length over which reaction occurs can be estimated and thus conversion obtained. Presence of unburned reactants in the exit stream may be due to this quenching behavior. Of course, for a more rigorous analysis of this situation it is necessary to analyze the solutions to the differential equations for three regions; i.e., no reaction, reaction, and again no reaction. This and the analysis of the related unsteady-state case involving in general third-order partial differential equations is being considered. The unsteady-state case is particularly interesting in relation to flashback and migration of ignition zones.

EXPERIMENTAL TEMPERATURE PROFILE

The validity of the temperature-profile expressions can be verified by use of the reactor

PART

12

Helene in New York, our Wedding and Life in Chicago

Helene came to New York in November 1951 on a military transport like us. Her aunt had come to New York a year earlier. They moved to Minneapolis six month later and lived there until her aunt's death in 1955. At her aunt's request my mother invited Helene to live with us in Brooklyn. She went to high school there and made many friends. Her best friend is Marie whom Helene still visits regularly in New York. We started dating shortly before I moved to Chicago. I spent most of my money traveling to Brooklyn to see my parents and Helene.

We were married in a Russian Orthodox Church in New York City. My groomsmen were friends from Brooklyn Poly and Chicago. Our wedding picture is shown in Figure 4.

Before we got married my mother invited my distant cousin Natasha from Paris to visit us and go to a popular beach In New Jersey. The swimming was excellent but unfortunately later on the beach got polluted.

In Chicago we lived near Lake Michigan first on Juneway Terrace and later on Sheridan Road.

Helene went to school at IIT part time and got a degree in mathematics which she found to be easy. She then earned a Master's degree in biochemistry at Roosevelt University. She had found a job at Illinois Masonic Hospital in the chemistry department. After working there for several years her boss Dr. Kelsey promoted her to be a supervisor.

Our son Misha was born at Illinois Masonic Hospital. Helene was working there the day he was born and went straight to the delivery room after work.

My parents had retired in Florida because my mother loved swimming and my father liked fishing. She took a bus almost every day to swim in the ocean. My father stayed home and smoked. He had a stroke and died in 1966.

In 1978 my mother came to live with us in Northbrook to help us take care of Misha while both us were working. We found a two story house in Northbrook with an in-law apartment for my mother and her friend whose wife had also died.

Helene found a position as supervisor of chemistry at Lutheran General Hospital which was closer to our house. All the staff liked Helene. A number of years later she was promoted to director of laboratories. As part of her job she visited many of the laboratories in Chicago and suburbs.

My mother died of colon cancer in our house in 1990. Both my parents are buried in Flagler Memorial Park in Miami, Florida.

Helene's job was eliminated when a new company took over the laboratories and she retired in 2001.

13

Teaching Chemical Engineering at IIT

After returning to IIT I was the program chairman for the 14th Energy Conversion Engineering Conference held in August 5-10,1979. Due to the energy crises, we had about 1,000 people attending the meeting and my phone rang non-stop. So I asked Hamid Arastoopour to be my co-chairman. He was excellent.

At IIT I taught mainly graduate courses, Transport Phenomena using Bird, Stewart and Lightfoot book, heat transfer and thermodynamics with Rob Selman. We had many part-time students, so we taught all the courses at night. We also had many chemistry students who wanted a degree in chemical engineering to get a higher paying job. At that time employers could deduct the tuition from their taxes. After Congress eliminated this deduction these students disappeared.

I had funding from the National Science Foundation to support mainly graduate students until my retirement.

Dr. Ojalvo of NSF helped me a lot. When one of my proposals did not get a good review, he said if I work with industry I will get funding. He suggested I work with EXXON in New Jersey. With an excellent PhD student from China we showed EXXON how to design one of their large reactors. The EXXON manager was pleased, but not the EXXON staff who used old fashioned methods.

When our chairman Darsh Wasan was promoted to a higher position, my former student from IGT Hamid Arastoopour became our chairman. He was an excellent chairman. When Hamid moved on to become dean of engineering, we hired Prakash from industry who almost destroyed our department. With funding hard to get due to the fact that it all went to the University of Chicago and the requirement to teach a new undergraduate course at night, I decided to retire. University of Chicago is a great school but they do not understand engineering. Under President Obama all our funding went to them, specifically to H.M.Jaeger who was a plenary lecturer at the World Congress on Particle Technology in 2018. The conclusion of his talk on contact charging of granular materials was that it is a difficult problem.

PART

14

My Trips and Lectures Worldwide

My first trip outside the USA was to Japan in 1964 and then around the world. Bernie Baker arranged for me to give a talk at a meeting on fuel cells and batteries in Japan and also in Paris. Two weeks before leaving there was an international conference in Chicago on heat transfer. There were many Russians attending. A professor of mechanical engineering, Kezios asked me to bring the Russians to his house where he was entertaining other overseas visitors. There I met the chairman of mechanical engineering from the University of Tokyo, the best university in Japan. Two weeks later I was in Tokyo and called him. He treated me to an excellent dinner and sent us several of his students.

From Japan I traveled to Paris. The plane stopped every two hours in the countries on the way. I visited my cousin Ala in Paris and my cousin Nina in Switzerland.

Mechanical engineering Professor Veziroglu organized a two week international conference in Turkey on multiphase flow, where I gave a presentation that the students applauded at the end. Helene and I stayed at the University. Charles Solbrig also came to the meeting with his wife Carol. Later Veziroglu organized many such conferences in Miami Beach, Florida. I gave presentations at most of those as well.

After I transferred to the chemical engineering department I still had to advise many students at IGT. For this Darsh Wasan obtained some money from IGT and put it into an account for me to spend on attending meetings. I used this money to go to England on their supersonic plane. Later I went to Thailand and recruited some good students to come to IIT. My contact in Thailand was Suchaya Nitivattananon. She was Hamid's PhD student and also my assistant in a course I was teaching. I usually gave no work to such assistants. This was a way for them to get money for living expenses. But Suchaya prepared her own examples and helped the students. Her thesis problem was very difficult because they did not have the right equipment. This reminded me of Schurig at Brooklyn Poly. I tried to help her.

At IIT I used to go swimming in the summer in Lake Michigan with one or two other professors. Suchaya organized our students to go with us. When her student Veeraya came to Chicago, she also went swimming with us. Suchaya went back to her university in Thailand to get a teaching job but there was a long waiting list. Later Suchaya came to IIT for a visit with her student Veeraya who later worked with me and came to our house in Northbrook for dinner almost every week. One time Ray Cocco, the director of PSRI met Veeraya at our house and found her a good job in industry. She worked for that company until she went back to Thailand to get married. Suchaya was my contact in Thailand. I went to their house, met her husband and her parents. She showed me around Bangkok.

Helene went with me to Thailand twice. She liked Bangkok very much. Chulalongkorn is the best university in Thailand. They sent us great students paid for by the King of Thailand. Their chairman took us to see the bridge on the river Kwai built by American and British captured soldiers. There is a special cemetery there for them. On the other side is a cemetery for the Japanese. There is some truth to the Hollywood movie, the King and I. Their king knew how to stay independent.

Our Trip to Phuket

Helene and I went to Phuket about one year after the destructive Tsunami on October 2,2018. The Thai government had cleaned up the destruction by the time we arrived. We stayed in a hotel up on a hill, had to take an elevator and cross a busy street to go swimming in the Pacific Ocean. On the beach Muslim women were selling excellent food. They were covered completely in a thin veil. One of the best activities in Phuket were the elephant rides. I could not control mine well but did not fall.

My Trip to Manaus

I was invited to teach a course in Brazil. On my return trip I stopped in Manaus, the old rubber capital of the world. This is where the Amazon River forms from convergence of the Negro River with the brown muddy Solimous River which is acid and therefor has no insects. I took a boat tour to go swimming in the Solimous River.

Our Trips to Brazil

I went to Brazil with Helene twice. The first time I was a guest lecturer at their annual engineering meeting. From Rio de Janeiro we traveled up a steep mountain to the meeting site. The town there looked like the Alps in Switzerland and the food was at least as good. I left shortly after my lecture because all the other presentations were in Portuguese.

During our second visit with Helene we stayed near the beach and went swimming in the Atlantic Ocean. There were armed guards patrolling the beach. We took a taxi to the Jesus Statue and climbed to the top to see the city below. Our hosts in Brazil warned us to be careful but said that the robbers only take your money if you do not resist. We had no problems only fun.

Our Trip to Australia

Helene and Misha accompanied me on a trip to a meeting in Australia in May 1992. On the way we stopped in Fiji where we snorkeled off the beach. We also saw a performance by the natives and drank their alcoholic brew. After a successful meeting we drove and then flew to Lady Elliot Island on the Great Barrier Reef. Hamid Arastoopour and his wife went with us. Today it is not allowed to go there because of the environmental threat to the reef.

My Trip to Norway

I taught a course at the Telemark Institute of Technology, Porsgrunn, Norway in 1992 and 1993. This was before my highly cited book, Multiphase Flow and Fluidization, Academic Press (1994) was published. They sent me a student Erik Manger who knew mathematics well. In 2001 with Lu Huilin's help we published a paper, kinetic theory of fluidized binary granular mixtures, Lu Huilin, D. Gidaspow and E. Manger, Physical Review E, vol 64,p 061301-1 to -8 (2001).

My Online Course

In 2008 I taught a course online in Finland at the Lappeenranta University of Technology. They are close to St. Petersburg, Russia, where my mother studied before WW2. This beautiful city was built by Peter the Great, a contemporary of Isaac Newton.

My First Trip to China

In 1984 through the National Science Foundation I went to China with several other professors from the USA to establish a working relationship with their universities. We first went to Xian to give our lectures and later to see the Terracotta Warriors nearby. In Xian we stayed in a large building built by the Russians with a gate and a guard. I went outside the gate and saw a lot of ladies selling Mau jackets. Suddenly they disappeared. A plain clothed policeman approached me and asked me what I wanted to buy illegally. I told him I was here to help China and went back inside the gate. He did not follow me. One of the Chinese professors from the meeting wanted to take me out for dinner. He was allowed to come into our compound.

China was a very poor country during President Reagan's time. We saw the Great Wall near Beijing. There was nothing to buy in the stores. One of the Chinese professors sent me his best student, J.Ding. With Ding we have 2 highly cited published papers, one with 2,000 citations (AIChE Journal 36,4,523-538.).

Lu Huilin

Lu Huilin came to work for me at IIT in 1995. We published several papers. He also made unique measurements at PSRI in their large fluidized bed that was shaking due to the large flow rate. In 1998 he went back to China to get his PhD degree.

In July 2004 Helene and I visited him in Harbin and went together to the Chinese Academy of Sciences in Beijing to give a talk. We also went sightseeing including the Great Wall. I got lost and had to ask the police to find Huilin and Helene who were shopping. Huilin and I developed a great working relationship. I am a co-author of many of his papers and we are trying to publish a book in China. I helped him get an award from AIChE. He works harder than anyone I have ever known.

2004, Great Wall of China

16

My Other Ph.D. Students at IIT

Here I describe the research of some of my PhD students who helped me with my own research.

1. Madhava Syamlal obtained his PhD in 1985 and worked for me for about 2 years. He helped me develop our CFD code. After DOE learned about our research Thomas O'Brien from Morgantown, West Virginia hired him. They developed the MFIX code which is an improvement of the Los Alamos K FIX code. Syamlal is now a Fellow at the National Energy Technology Laboratory in Pittsburg. He has 6400 citations in Google Scholar, a very high number. He is working on quantum computing that promises to be very fast and small. China has invested more money into the project than the USA. Quantum computing may help us find out how the virus gets into the human cells and therefore develop vaccines for future viruses.

2. Isaac Gamwo came to us from Cameroon. His father was a king there and Isaac is the oldest son. I found this out only after he had to go to Africa after his father died. Isaac did his PhD work at the Argonne National Lab with Bob Lyczkowski. I helped them get a contract from NETL on erosion in fluidizid beds. Isaac did 90% of the work. After he became a US Citizen he got a job at DOE NETL in Pittsburg. He is now a Fellow there. I worked with Isaac for two summers. We filed a joint patent, US 7,619,011 B1,Nov 17,2009.

3. Aubrey Miller was a football player in Michigan. After graduation he briefly worked in industry and then came to get a PhD at IIT. He chose me as his advisor. For his PhD thesis he built a two story circulating fluidized bed in Perlstein hall and made unusual measurements with a moving probe. Circulating fluidized beds have the property of operating at a nearly constant temperature despite a large heat generation. He did not need much help from me. We published his paper in 1962. See A. Miller, and D. Gidaspow, Dense Vertical Gas-Solid Flow in a Pipe, AIChE Journal 38,1801-1815. Our CFB is also shown in great detail in the book by D. Gidaspow and V. Jiradilok Nova (2009).

Miller taught at IIT for one year, was very well liked by our students and then went to teach at the University of West Virginia. There the department of energy had a lab with a circulating fluidized bed much poorer than the one Miller had built at IIT. Unfortunately the dean of engineering did not give Miller tenure because he told him that his research was poor. I told Miller that his paper and one more without me were better than all the engineering papers published in chemical engineering in West Virginia. His paper with me had about 100 citations already. He sued the university and won but he was out of a job. R.W.Brealt of DOE-NETL gave Miller a contract to take data similar to that he took at IIT. Brealt said Miller is the only one he trusted to obtain such data. Much later Brealt came to Chicago to find students as good as Miller. There were none.

4. Augusto Neri came to us from Italy to do his PhD thesis under my direction. In a short time we published two highly cited papers, A.Neri and D. Gidaspow, AIChE Journal 46(1),52-67 and A.Neri, et al, Journal Geophysical Research: Solid Earth 108(B4). Neri came to visit us several times. He has a chapter in our book, Transport Phenomena in Multiphase Systems, H.Arastoopour, D.Gidaspow & R.W. Lyczkowski,Springer Verlag,2021.

5. York P.Tsuo and I published our highly cited paper based on his PhD Thesis, computaton of flow patterns in circulating fluidized beds, AIChE Journal 36(6),885-896.

   York formed his own company to make silicon for solar collectors. I was hired as a consultant and filed 2 provisional patents. It was fun working with his people because I solved their problems very quickly. After York hired a manager it became impossible to work there. York sold his company to the Chinese.

6. Reza Mostofi did his PhD under my direction. He linked our FORTRAN program to graphical user interphase to make plots, movies, to obtain averages, etc. This software was written in MATLAB and made data analysis very easy. We published a highly cited paper with Bill Koves from UOP, Jiradilok et al Chemical Eng. Science 61(17)5544-5559.

   Reza got a job at UOP in Des Plaines. He directs all of UOP simulations. UOP and EXXON-MOBIL helped us win WW2 by creating proper fuels for our airplanes which the Germans did not know how to do. I had worked with EXXON and helped them scale-up one of their reactors.

   I used to go to lunch with Reza very often and hope to go again after the COVID 19 epidemic is over.

7. Susan J.Gelderbloom worked for a company in Midland, Michigan. Her boss organized a 5 member team to solve the CFD problem. I was a member of the team. We all met at the university locations. I showed 50 people our two story circulating fluidized bed. The people from Los Alamos came to see it. They had a running CFD code but had difficulty running it and were mad at me when I wanted to compare their results to ours.

   Susan's company paid us travel expenses and for our time through the universities. Susan wanted to get a PhD degree. She drove to IIT once a week to talk to me. She did a number of useful experiments and some theory.

   The company did not permit her to put her experiments into her thesis. To write a paper based on her thesis Bob Lyczkowski drove to Michigan with me. Our paper was published in the AIChE Journal, 49(4)844-858,S.J Gelderbloom, D. Gidaspow and RW Lyczkowski. At the same time Susan got her PhD at IIT her son graduated from West Point.

8. Mateo Strumendo from Italy came to work with me . At that time I had insufficient funding so he worked for Hamid Arastoopour instead. He spent a lot of time at our house. When his parents came to visit him we invited them to dinner. His father had been in charge of Northern Italy. When our son worked in Italy for two years, Mateo's father was very helpful with some bureaucratic issues.

9. Mehmet Tartan eliminated the use of a probe for taking data in our riser. See Tartan, M and D. Gidaspow, Measurement of Granular Temperature and Stresses in Risers, AIChE Journal 50,1760-1775.

We find that the solid volume distribution is as follows:

$$2/3 \, \varepsilon_s \, /\{1- [r/R\}^{4]}$$

where R is the pipe radius and r is the radial dimension, ε is the volume fraction and s stands for the solids. See page 332,

Computational Techniques, D.Gidaspow and V.Jiradilok, Nova, 2009.

Mehmet is working for General Motors. He went to China several times on business.

10. Mayank Kashyap and his wife Teresita are now working in Houston. They both obtained their PhD degrees from IIT. I have several papers published with Mayank, for example, M. Kashyap & D. Gidaspow, Computation and measurements of mass transfer and dispersion coefficients in fluidized beds, Powder Technology 203 (1),40-56.

Mayank is very active in AIChE. He helped to create an award for young professionals. He is working for a Saudi Arabian company in Houston. He and his family have visited us numerous times.

17

IIT Research Institute

IIT research institute, IITRI was working with the military before I was born. They had a testing station in Michigan when I worked with them. They hosted seminars every year in Colorado. William Comeyne from Belvoir Research and Development Center in Fort Belvoir, Virginia was the sponsor of IITRI research. He wanted to see some models of their experiments. That is how I got involved in their research. We first simulated an explosion of TNT into a large bag done at their testing station. The simulation was done with the help of my PhD student, M. Syamlal. At IITRI my supervisor was James L. Austing. He told me what simulations to do and was not interested in my suggestions of how to make improvements. His boss was Allen J. Tullis. Later I got several PhD students involved in the simulations.

The first was David F. Aldis. We published our papers in the AIChE Journal in July 1990,36.1087-1096, two-dimensional analysis of a dust explosion and combustion of polydispersed solids using a particle population balance, Powder Technology 57,281-194 (1989),

The second PhD student was Ron Pape. We modeled the velocity, volume fractions and the temperature of a new rocket motor to explain why it functions better than the usual rockets. Our paper was presented at the American Society of Mechanical Engineers, Vol 238.

In 1990 U.K. Jayaswal developed a model for dissemination into the IITRI bag. As a result of this excellent study he got hired to work on missile defense. His work was used to protect Israel from missiles.

The most comprehensive paper on our work at IITRI is described in the PhD thesis of Veeraya Jiradilok from Thailand with her PhD advisors, Suchaya Nitivattanon, Somsak Damronglerd and myself published in Powder Technology 163,33-39 (2006).

I also worked with IITRI on mine neutralization and during the Reagan presidency on missile defense. IITRI got a large contract with the Boeing company. But once they learned what we were doing they cancelled the IITRI contract. In the meanwhile IITRI had stopped working on Fort Belvoir research. Comeyne came to complain, but IITRI did not listen. I asked Darsh Wasan for his advice and he said it was not my problem. Now IITRI had no funding and had to lay off all their staff. The IIT President collected a salary from IITRI but did not help them. Our chemical engineering department lost future graduate students paid by IITRI. Unfortunately our board of directors did not understand the IITRI problem.

During the Trump administration there was interest in how to shoot down missiles from North Korea. I submitted my idea. It generated a lot of interest but I could not find anyone with a high security clearance to work with me.

18

Teaching After Retirement

I retired at end of the year in 2009.The reason was that due to some friction in our department we hired J Prakash from industry to be our chairman. He did not understand how universities function and ordered me to teach new undergraduate courses late at night. As a Distinguished Professor I was allowed to teach courses of my choice. I was elected Distinguished Professor in the year 2000 because of my many acomplishments, such as an award from von Brown for improving fuel cells for moon landing, my now highly cited book, Multiphase Flow and Fluidization, the Kern award for heat transfer and other professional awards.

I made my choice to retire without a protest because I had an interesting part-time job in industry. My former PhD student York Tsuo had a company to make polysilicon for solar cells using fluidized beds. It was fun working there with young professionals who wanted my help to design their unit. Unfortunately when York hired a manager my contributions were not recognized. I filed two provisional patents described in our Springer 2021 book, Transport Phenomena in Multiphase Systems by H. Arastoopour, D.Gidaspow and Robert W. Lyszkowski,edited by Frank Kulacki, my former MS student at IGT. Frank was Dean of Engineering most of his life. Recently he was an editor of many Springer books.

After retirement I was allowed to teach only in the summer at IIT in an auditorium where my lectures were recorded. I used our book with Veeraya Jiradilok, Computational Techniques,2009, Nova. Every student had to do his own problem and present his solution. At first there were many students but slowly the number of students decreased, as the number of PhD students dropped.

I stopped teaching altogether after I was diagnosed with prostate cancer. I am now recovering slowly under the care of urologist Dr. Mutchnik. Following medical guidelines my primary care physician Dr. Steven Eisenstein stopped doing annual PSA's in 2011 because of my age. Between 2011 and 2020 my PSA rose from 5.18 to greater than 2000. A healthy man has a PSA of zero. In 2011 I was only 77 years old and was very active.

The good news for our department is that we now have an excellent chairman, Sohail Murad. Unlike some previous chairmen, he listens to suggestions. For example he brought up for faculty consideration my suggestion of giving only open book exams. Like Dr. Peck I did that and often assigned each student a different problem. Sohail also invited a former student of ours, Tulsi Tawari to give a talk on engineering economics. He published a book, Creation of wealth vs. transfer of wealth. Investment in infrastructure according to Keynes theory leads to a large wealth creation. According to Tulsi our moon program led to a recovery of $1,000 for every dollar we invested. I am working with Tulsi on a book that will have a generalization of Keynes theory.

The chemical engineering Peck seminars and our other seminars are a unique feature of our department. They are well-attended by faculty and students.

19

Bob Lyczkowski

When I worked in Idaho with Bob and Charlie Solbrig Bob drove to Sacramento to visit my friend from New York George Kostyrko. After a short visit we drove to visit Bob's friends in Livermore.

In 1993 we taught a 5 day course in Melbourne, Australia at CSIRO. Bob rented a car and drove us to CSIRO facilities and swimming in the ocean. Our course was on fluidized beds similar to the one I taught in Norway, but now teaching with Bob made it much easier for me. Later Bob organized a Festschrift in my honor, published in June 2, 2010 in I&EC Research Vol 49. He also organized AIChE meetings in my honor that were well attended by my friends and those interested in computational fluid dynamics. In our department at IIT he created two fellowships in my name and persuaded friends and former students to contribute.

We have remained close friends. We often talk on the phone and before the pandemic Bob was a frequent visitor at our house. We also enjoyed going out for dinner and for draft beer especially at Hackneys. We hope to do it again soon.

I spent about 2 years full-time working with Bob on our book, Transport Phenomena in Multiphase Systems by

H. Arastoopour, D.Gidaspow and R.W. Lyczkowski, Springer Verlag,2021. Bob is a pleasure to work with.

Both Bob an I read a lot of books. Bob checks them out from a good library near Argonne National Lab. Helene buys them for me at the Book Bin near us. We often discuss the books we are reading. A fascinating book I have read recently is one recommended by Bob. It is by M.J. Neufeld, Von Braun (Vintage Books,2007). Without the Russian's Sputnick and Von Braun we would not have gone to the moon. I knew all this before reading the book. I did not know that Von Braun was from a landowning family in Prussia, that he had met Hitler more than once and that he called himself a rocket engineer. He is in this sense similar to the physicist Robert Oppenheimer who managed the building of the atomic bomb in Los Alamos. For every dollar we spent on the moon program we got one thousand dollars back. The science of building the atomic bomb is similar to that of building nuclear reactors that produced inexpensive power for a short time but will cost us too much in the long run.

Appendix 1

Deepwater Horizon Oil Spill

Our Explanation

The reason that this disaster happened is that there was at that time nobody on the vessel who understood how to pump the oil. The government regulators in Houston did not understand the process of deep sea drilling. We simulated the first few minutes of the oil spill as described in our paper, D .Gidaspow, F. Li and J. Huang, A CFD simulator for multiphase flow in reservoirs and pipes, Powder Technology, 242, 2-12 (2013) and at the 2011 AIChE meeting in Minneapolis, October 16-21, 2011. I was hired as a consultant by BP to give an expert opinion in their case. This was cancelled when the government settled the case.

Appendix 2

Kinetic Theory of Blood Flow

The papers by D.Gidaspow and J. Huang, Annals of Biomedical Engineering (2009) and that by D.Gidaspow, Y.He and V.Chandra Chemical Eng. Science 134,784-799 (2015) show how to compute the migration of red blood cells from the center to the walls creating a red blood cell free space. The platelets move toward the walls helping the healing of cuts.

The approximate analytical solution for the platelet concentration, n is given by

$$n/\text{inlet } n = 1/ \{1- (r/R))^{1/4}$$

where R is the tube radius and r is the radial coordinate.

This concentration can be related to the LDL concentrations. and hence its importance.

Appendix 3

Infrastructure

The Sunday August 7, 2016 New York Times article asks the question: where did all the growth go?

It shows that between 1980 and 2005 the US growth was 2%. In 2005 the GDP dropped to -7% due to the rush to lend money to homeowners without regard for their ability to pay. Wall street discovered a new kind of mortgage for borrowers who could not repay the money they borrowed.

About 1,000 salesmen sold such houses to people who could not afford them. These salesmen eventually went to jail for not checking to see whether the buyers had the ability to pay back the loans, while the big crooks on wall street went free.

The 1532 book by Nikollo Machiavelli, The Prince based on historical facts, describes how a ruler must govern. He must take into consideration that a human being is both an angel and a wild beast.

Karl Marx and Engels did not take into account the nature of humans. Thus communism in both Russia under Stalin and in China under Mau after WW2 produced poverty and death. Today China is a rich country because of regulated capitalism with more economic equality than we have in the USA.

In chemical and mechanical engineering we teach students how to make balances of mass, momentum and energy, but not money. A long time ago we used Samuelson's book in economics. It is based on Keynes theory. The system is a nation.

The mathematical balance is :

Rate of accumulatio + net rate of outflow of money = rate of money creation.

In the balance we need to define money. There is more than one definition of money. The most common definition is in Wikipedia. Money is record for payment of goods and services. A different definition will lead to different results.

Infrastructure Investment

Construction of the Interstate highway system in the USA under President Eisenhower is an example of a wise investment. *Keynes (1936) theory supported by data shows that for every dollar invested by federal government we get back two or more dollars. The Chinese went much further in their own and other countries.* They saved Greece by rebuilding the port of Athens.

We let our bridges, trains, etc deteriorate for decades. In China some of their trains use magnetic levitation and are now faster than the bullet trains in Japan. Such construction in the USA now would provide badly needed jobs and wealth creation. Hopefully the Biden administration will build such infrastructure and make this country the greatest in the world again.

Government investment into vaccination is also wealth creation, since people will go back to work, restaurants will reopen, etc.

Appendix 4

Improved Keynes Theory

Keynes theory was criticized by University of Chicago professors for not being complete. Here is our improvement with the addition of private investment, P which can be positive or negative.

In Keynes theory we have :

Y(t)=National income at time, t

C(t)=Consumption at time, t

I(t)=Investment at time, t

G(t)=Government investment at time, t

P = Private investment

Then, Y(t)=C(t)+I(t)+G(t)+P

In Keynes theory we assume

C(t)=a Y(t-1)

I(t)=b{C(t)-C(t-1}

where a and b are unknown constants in the second order finite difference equation that are obtained from data, such as GDP growth rate in the USA. In 1932 GDP was -13% and in 1934 it went to 11% . These numbers in Keynes theory show that for every dollar invested in putting people to work we get ten dollars back.

With private investment of P dollars the national income rises by P dollars more than that in the Keynes theory.

When in the USA houses were sold to people who could not afford them, P was negative.

Appendix 5

White Evangelicals

When I was in high school in New York my mother sent me to a Christian camp for vacation. There were boys and girls in dorms far apart. We had to listen to evangelical preachers 3 times a day. They preached from the old testament. One of them said that when we go to college and study geology, on the exam we should write what we were taught, but add that we do not believe this to be the truth.

Jimmy Carter in his book, Faith (2018) describes his experience with one of the evangelical leaders in Georgia after he came home from the Navy. Their leader asked him to join them. When Carter refused he told everyone that Carter is a communist and that no one should buy their peanuts. Carter eventually convinced them that this was false.

I first learned about Carter from a New York Times article, "The Peanut Farmer".

In the Navy Carter helped to develop the first nuclear submarine. As our President he prevented the release of radiation from the Three Mile Island Unit 2 nuclear reactor near Midletown,

Pa. He came to look at the reactor and listened to input of many people including my PhD student, Charles Solbrig . They suggested to pressurize the reactor which was counterintuitive but it worked.

The book, His very Best, by J. Alter, Simon & Schuster, 2020, describes many of Carter's accomplishments as President and very briefly why he lost the election to Reagan.

Appendix 6

Timeshare in Mexico

We bought a one bedroom apartment in Mexico for a week. We first went to Nueva Vallarta on the Pacific Ocean to find calm waters for swimming. It is a 4 and 1/2 hour flight from Chicago.

Helene would walk to a small town nearby, called Bucerias which has a large open air market and many restaurants. In the evening we would take a taxi for dinner. One time we went on a whale watching tour and one of the whales came right to our boat.

Later we started going to Cancun on the Caribbean Sea. Our resort is opposite Isla Mujeres which has a restaurant that serves the best whole red snapper I have ever eaten. We took a large ferry which docks walking distance form our hotel. The best meal at the resort is their breakfast buffet. The fresh fruit is first rate. Such fruit cannot be found in the USA. The dinners are expensive and their quality is not consistent. Our resort is at the edge of Cancun and therefore the taxis to go to the center of town are expensive. Swimming in the ocean and a large pool is excellent.

Appendix 7

Climate Change

At IGT we worked on a problem of transferring CO_2 for a molten carbonate fuel cell from one electrode to another. In 1975 we obtained a patent with my PhD student Mike Onischak. See our highly cited patent, D. Gidaspow and M. Onischak, U.S. Patent 3,865,924.

A similar problem occurs in submarines where the carbon dioxide is captured and stored. Our sorbent can be regenerated with low level heat and therefore can be used to remove the carbon dioxide from the atmosphere.

This will help with climate change.

Thank You Helene

I thank Helene for her suggestions.

Printed in the United States
by Baker & Taylor Publisher Services